IN MY HEAD

Sinéad Hoben

For Stan, Tara, Sarah, Jack and Sophia

'Poetry is when an emotion has found its thought and the thought has found words.'

ROBERT FROST

CONTENTS

FOREWORD

During the Covid-19 pandemic, my husband once re-marked he would not like to live inside my head as, to him, it appears a dark place. Plagued by anxiety, I often agreed. This wasn't helped when I was diagnosed with early breast cancer in April 2021 and underwent sur-gery... However, my love of words helped me through some of my worst days and ultimately led to this book, so, in my defence, inside my head there is also a lot of com-fort to be had!

I hope you, dear reader, enjoy my work, and recognise some of yourself in the poems. My words bring light into the darkness for me, and I hope they do the same for you.

PROLOGUE

I write,
I become,
The mist retreats.
I am done.

A NEW WORLD

Like a child's toy,
Spinning through Space and Time,
Unsullied, unspoilt,
Until populated,
They polluted me.

Now I shrug,
And soon they'll be gone
And once again
I'll spin and I'll dance
Into the darkness and into the
light...

GRATITUDE

A paperback book,
A little pink bike,
Motionless footballs side by side!
Sun dappled leaves casting shadows
On me,
As reclined,
I enjoy
A warm hug of bliss
In my garden.

FACE

My son's face
Smiles at me
From a time before
He or I was born.
Family genes
Looking at me
From an old photograph
That was torn
In half,
Then taped back together,
Escorting the past
Into now.

MISTS

Thunder was forecast,
But didn't come for us.
Instead I awoke,
In sunrise hours,
To satin mist,
Like Autumn dropping by
On a Summer's day,
Gifting me
Welcome refreshments beyond
The paned window,
Dew clinging
To grassy tips and succulent leaves,
As birds chirp contentedly
In cool, damp air.

FULL STOP

Insignificant beetle!
You crawl across my page
A mobile punctuation mark,
Pausing periodically,
Mid line,
Composing nonsensical sentences.
Tiny, delicate
I could smudge you
Out.
A gentle breath
Dispenses you.
My roaming full stop,
You are gone.

VIRUS

Silently, skilfully,
From one host to another,
Striking fear into
Father, mother,
Sister, brother,
The Enemy declares War.

Unseen.

Fighting blind,
We cannot run;
It's everywhere,
And everyone.
Is this the end?
Or has our battle
Just begun?
Somewhere, lurking,
There is another one.

THE GIFT

Snakelike, an uninvited guest
Shrouds me in fear.

My birthday,
A day of fun
Cake, candles, gifts,
Usually...
But today
My unwelcome guest smirks at me,
Threateningly.
I can't tell if he will
Run his cold clawing slime through my
veins,
I can't tell when or if he'll strike:
Fear is his to give.

His Gift:
Appreciation.

Oh to go for a long walk in woody
forests,
Oh to kiss my child's soft silky skin,
To sit in a park
Drinking in joyous
Children squealing delightfully.
Oh to stop and stand close to a par
ent, Neighbour, friend,

Chatting.
Oh to tightly hug,
Or shake a friendly hand,
Carelessly visit shops, cafes,
The seaside   picnic ready!

When this ends
His will not lie unwanted, unused:
It will be treasured
A parting gift my undesired guest
Slipped quietly into my heart.

And I will share it with all the
world.

NAMES

In awkward conversation,
I might let slip a name
To which a smile twinkles
And a voice glitters,
'You are probably related.'

Living on an island,
The likelihood was always high,
And it didn't bode well for teenage love!

Years later and perhaps
It's inevitable
That I sing the same song.
Rolled eyes and exasperated sighs
As I become my mother
But now I understand
The essence of her words.

DESTINATION: SOMEWHERE

Honking overhead

3 crows

Like lorry drivers

Greet one another

Mid air.

From my sun lounger

I note the black sheen of their
underbellies

And watch each glide purposefully

Onwards.

Never have I known

They glance left and right

Mid flight

Air traffic control,

Observed from below,

As each courses towards

Destination: Somewhere.

MAGPIE MURDER

On a hot sunny day,
With a locked down world relaxing,
I heard the commotion,
Observed a flurry of motion,
From my garden chair.
I heard the frantic squeals
Of a panicked mother.
Towering over her,
A beast with pin eyes,
Challenging.
Tightly clutched in sharp talons,
Your knife beak stabbing,
Your monster claws shredding,
Her nest stolen chick.
She begged you:
Stop.
Cried for others:
Help.
But you destroyed her offspring
Even, as painfully,
The chick chirped.
I stood up,
A witness to murder,
Helpless,
As prey in claw,

You flew to a chimney pot,
Your murderous mission
Complete.
After,
Perched on the rooftop,
The mother bird
Despondent.
Her chick's remains
A chimney stain,
And she called and called,
But no one came.

CHAT, CONVERSATION, END

A passing word,
A quick chat,
Or full conversation.
Words spill out.
With every turn
Of phrase,
The face changes.
A scowl,
A frown,
A smile or grin,
Sometimes just within.
Recipients listen,
With feigned appreciation
Or not.
Bore,
Genius,
Friend,
Foe.
Words flow.
People melding
Into memories of all the words
Left behind.

INSIDE OUT

Looking outside,
From the safety of my bed,
All looks well
As far as I can tell

Blue skies are calling,
Green trees are blowing,
But I'm trapped inside
And my world is slowing.

The future looks uncertain,
From behind my bedroom curtain,
But one day I'm sure this will be
All behind me.

HOPE

Caterpillar of hope,
Creeping quietly,
Alongside the silent harbour wall,
Your inspiring words
Hope, Serenity, Love,
Lift fear soaked
Passersby.
You give us purpose:
To keep working together,
To keeping moving onwards,
Despite the drag of fear,
Pulling us back.
Your movement,
Slow and steady,
Grounds us,
Helps us face the storm brewing,
As you promise brighter, lighter,
Future days.

BEDTIME

Little bare feet,
Racing upstairs.
Teeth, PJs,
A story and prayers;
Every night
A well polished show.

The joyful leap into bed:
Cuddly toys removed, replaced,
Re positioned with care.

Curtains drawn,
Bedding down,
And the gentle glow
Of a bedside lamp,
As a sleepy head imprints on a pillow.

The goodnight,
The love you,
The sleep tight
Whispered,
As the door closes softly.

Another generation,
Enjoying the bedtime routine.

COMMUNION

Uno, Spanish for one.
Communion,
The priest explained,
Is Oneness,
What Christ becomes
With us.
First Communion:
A precious day,
A lifelong memory.
Preceding preparations:
First Confession, Prayers,
Shopping excitedly
For dresses, veils, shoes, suits.
Families
Celebrating
The creation
Of unification.

Postponed.

Covid 19
Keeping us apart
First Holy Communion,
Confirmation,
Weddings,

Special days,
All on pause.
Funerals unstoppable,
Mourners reduced.

But, we fight back:
The Communion of Humans
Cannot be stopped,
Coming together apart,
To work together,
To celebrate together.
An invisible web of
Technology,
Keeping us unified,
Until together,
We safely meet.
Community in Unity.

Uno.

COVID LOVE

(For Tara)

Side by side,
Purposefully they stride,
Together as one,
Towards a bus
Neither wants to catch.
Forbidden hands
Clutched together
Readying themselves for
Another long goodbye.

SAME

Today: same as yesterday.

Tomorrow: same as today.

Same birds sing,

Same dogs bark,

Same people,

Same strangers,

Treading same paths.

The familiar unknown?

Same...

COFFEE

Dreaming a different life,
A known scent
Fills the fantasy as
That wondrous world
Mists over.

Still closed eyes
Struggle to open,
Flickering to the real...
And there it sits,
Ready to savour.

Silent hands,
Deliverers to the doorstep
Of my dream
Are gone
But the welcome silky liquid
Brings life into focus,
As moment by moment,
I become me once more.

PEACE

A pencil scratches across a silent page,
A message hastily delivered.
The warm hum of central heating
Blends
With the gentle lull
Of a laptop fan.
Muffled voices rise and fall
From rooms above and beyond,
As outside,
A silent wind
Rustles fruitful hedges,
And colourful trees
Jingle summer clothing.
Sweeping above,
Fluffy clouds embark
On a journey unknown.

Swooping in formation,
A flock of birds
Circle overhead.
All the while
I watch and listen,
My soul relaxing
Into cosy bliss.

SUN LOUNGING

Reclining on a sun warmed chair,
The golden heat of sunshine
Beats upon my head
As distant traffic buzzes
Towards unknown destinations
Whilst a butterfly flutters
On a static bicycle wheel and
Busy bees suckle on grass grown
clover.
The radio news sounds on the hour;
Stories from afar
Landing on my doorstep.

Another summer's day:
Warm breeze
On hot hair,
Skin glistening...

Reluctantly,
I retreat indoors
The respite of a cool house
Enticing me.

WEDDING ANNIVERSARY

(For my parents)

Golden years shimmering
With nurtured memories,
Sunlight haloed roses
Perfuming the air.
Smiles beaming
As once newly weds
Celebrate anew;
Fifty cherished years
As one.

VIRTUAL SPORTS DAY

All the usual fun and games
But not the same;
A solitary smiling face,
Alone in a race,
In a grassy garden,
Not a school field.
Still competing,
And completing,
Following the rules,
In broken ranks.
The fun, the laughter,
The ever after,
The one they'll remember
In times to come,
That happened alone.
A virtual sports day
Partaken at home...

FORBIDDEN HUGS

my daughter in front of me
recoils visibly
fearfully
as
my arms sweep open
almost embracing
needing
hoping
but hugs are forbidden
as elbow bumps
replace
but don't
suffice.

our eyes fill
tearfully
as we bid our goodbyes
and deeply sad
we part again
hoping soon to hold each other tight.

the pain of pandemic life
real life
now.

REMEMBERING HOLIDAYS

The booking, the planning,
Home leaving, then driving,
The arriving, the unpacking,
Day tripping, photographing.
Memory making, much laughing,
More packing, departing.
The wonderful homecoming,
The end of holidaying
Until next year
Harks another vacation!

PIANO

(For Sophia)

Tinkling on piano keys,
My 8 year old daughter
Plays a tune,
Then announces she has
Learned it all
So soon!
Just one day it took her
To master the instrument
New to her:
Oh the sweet confidence
Of Childhood.

LESSONS

Pitter patter of tiny feet,
Eyes shining bright
As mine they meet,
Questions many every day,
A world of Wonder
To take away...

SATURDAY

Saturday morning,
Fresh and bright,
Awakening from restful sleep,
I lie restless.
Stepping gently
On the cool floor,
I remove myself
From that sacred stillness
And downstairs quietly tread,
Hopeful for coffee and
Brief time alone,
Before the bustle
Of family life
Arises anew.

SUMMER SNOW STORM

Like delicate snow flakes
The petals of the firethorn fall,
Rushes of white
Floating and twirling
In the light of a sun filled corner,
Dappling grass with
The gentlest June blizzard.

A perfect summer storm.

ROSE PETALS

Pink red velvet rose petals
Litter my feet,
Their streaked veins
No longer
Life giving.

With every breeze,
Another drops with a soft
Thud.

Never was garden loss
So pretty
A grass bath,
Petals afloat,
Sunshine glinting
Off dew topped tips.

IRONY

Ironically,
I've never much liked
Poetry
And yet I find
I'm most inclined
To relax into it
Gently.
I find a spot
And let my mind
Roam free,
Letting words
Twist and meld,
And find myself
Revelling
In capturing
Fleeting moments
Of aforementioned
Poetry.

FATHER'S DAY

(For Dad)

It was different this year
As gifts of beer,
Chocolate and cards
Were presented from a
Socially acceptable distance.

No hugs were given
As they're still forbidden,
But love flows free
The bond unbroken
Between my father and me.

GIFTGIVING

(For Mum)

Handing over my gift
Without customary hugs
Felt wrong.
A deep melancholy
Shared between us
That love is different
Not forever,
Just for now.

ANOTHER SLEEPLESS NIGHT

I awaken from a dream
Close to reality
A cat hair in my
Eye,
But not really!
The silent house creaks
As I wander downstairs
To the beeps of security
Which I rush to silence.
Soon, a bubbling kettle,
The promise of tea.
Drawing room dark curtains,
A soft mist calls me outdoors,
Drink in hand.
Morning damp air cools me,
As alone in Nature,
I breathe this moment.

I sit,
Sun lit in my
Rose draped corner.
A collared dove observes from
The rooftop,
Neck cocked,
As do I

Back at him.
The dawn chorus
Chirps and squeaks,
Cars beyond roar and pass.
Life   an early start for some.
For me, this morning
Soothes and comforts,
A new day,
Life's journey continues.

DEW

Morning Dew
Clings to rose leaves,
Grass and trees;
A promised drip
Of Life inverted
In a small bubble burst.

DAISY

Cool morning air,
A daisy yearns
Towards where
The sun should be.
Cloaked in mist,
Desired light
Hidden,
The little sun shine flower
Waves gently
Hopeful
Of reflected light
Later.

BIRDSONG

Where are they all,
Those hidden birds
That cheep and chirp
Dusk and Dawn?
I hear their sounds
All around,
But none I see
Their musical chorus
Concealed
From me.

BED

Cocooned from the world,
In softened light,
I awaken,
Hazy.
Motionless,
I lie listening.
An early riser
Downstairs goes through
Morning motions:
Kettle boiling,
Coffee bean grinding
The pungent powder
Spooned into place.
A robot vacuum
Journeys a room,
Breakfasting on yesterday's debris.
Far off traffic buzzing
Companionably
To the drone
Of a neighbouring
Lawnmower
As day breaks through
Curtained windows.
I rise to the call
Of birdsong,

And life begins
Again.

SEA

The slosh and slap
Of rolling waves on rocks,
As somewhere above,
An unseen seabird
Shrieks and swoops,
And dusk draws close.

WARRENPOINT

Glinting sun
On shifting tides,
Chameleon waters
Partnering a
Soft sea breeze:
Today's troubles
Soothed away,
Wave by rolling wave...

WINE

Ruby red,
I sip you in
And swirl you around.

Like a joyous dancer,
Gracefully you glide over
Tastebuds that tingle delightfully.

Sweet welcome bitterness
Floods me;
You waterfall my depths
Releasing expectantly
The slow and steady
Hit of relaxed giddiness.

It's hard to beat
Rioja!

DEPTHS

Like deep rivers,
Muddied thoughts
Stream,
Dreamlike,
Blurring vision,
Dulling sounds,
The future culled
Uncertain.

Ahead,
I cannot see.
Bright days
Will return,
They say,
As birds chirp free
Their hopeful songs this
Miserable day.

Spring abounds,
And with it,
Light.
But
Far away
The future feels today.
I will stoke my

Embers of Hope
And my fire will burn bright
Tomorrow.

2020

I never imagined
I'd share a pandemic
With the world.
But here we are,
Together:
Surviving.
The odds are good,
Apparently!
Yet fear paralyses
And deprives us
Of life previous.
With one another,
Socially distanced
In our new world,
We'll find a way to
Get by and survive it.

That's how life works now;
It's how we'll get through
This.
Pandemic: no panic.
Tell my head that!

SHOPPING

Today I face
My Covid fear,
Mask faced,
I traipse
The empty aisles,
Missing smiles
Of yesterday.
People pass,
No one asks,
'How are you?'
This time is strange,
Life has changed,
And will again
For better,
Not worse!

Now where's my purse?

SOPHIA

Suddenly,
It happened
My little girl
Made toast
On her own!
Buttered and plated,
And I could see
Clearly,
No longer the baby,
Not quite a big girl,
But independent and free,
She is becoming of me.
This small child,
My youngest one
(A little pleasure,
A gentle treasure),
Is growing fast
Within our home.

FRUSTRATION

Moans and groans,
Meaningful sighs and
Impassioned eyes,
Frustration played out
On the keyboard.
Yet she persists,
Time and again,
Learning to master
Which notes come after,
As she teaches herself piano.

TOGETHER

(For Stan)

Together we sleep,
Together we dream,
Our life as one
Is all that it seems.
Together we love,
Together we grow,
Our life with each other,
We've made it so.

BEACH DAY

The sea, the spray,
The ball, the play,
The sun, the light
Oh so bright!
The wind,
Like breath,
The air
So cold
My hands
Are numb!
I head
Back home
To heat
And sleep
And memories
That flood
My blood.

SPRING

Springtime beckons
With the gentlest wave
As cool evening air
Paves her way.

Roadside daffodils on
Slender stalks sway,
Budding leaves
Paint a frieze
On bushes and trees,
As crocuses dot barren land.

A child's voice,
Out of sight,
Blends with the noise
Of birdsong
In stretched evening light.

Those in the know,
Rejoice and proclaim,
That Summer will
Return soon again.

PARAMEDICS

Numbness cloaks
My shoulders,
Lightly, veil like.
Calmly, this moment surreal,
I'm guided,
Not knowing if
I'll return.
Gentle hands lead
My way
As I, in peace,
Surrender.
I survive:
Night, then day.
Another chance,
I hold tight.
To Life.

EMERGENCY

High on morphine,
Flat on my back,
The Ambulance
Raced through the night.

Blind to the roads,
I relaxed and conversed,
As corners were
Taken at speed.

The paramedic calmly
Queried my life,
Revealing hers in
Return

A life planned out
From 5 years old,
Never veering,
Or steering off course.

All the time,
Her eyes on mine,
Smiling and
Keeping me calm.
Briefly glancing a screen

Above me,
Occasionally halting mid line
She adjusted, reviewed, reassured.

At 27 a first time mother was I,
Protecting my newborn,
Protecting me on this fateful encoun
ter,
A girl the age of my daughter.

Finally, we arrived
At our destination,
Pain controlled and
Journey complete.

Into the night
My companion
Fled
On to save another.

PAIN

Tonight,
17 years ago,
In labour I struggled
Before my baby was born:
The current pain familiar,
The solitary overnight bag,
This time, no baby reward.

All around in A&E,
Sounds of anguish,
Ingratitude,
Hacking coughs,
Banter,
And laughter.

A night familiar to nurses,
Doctors,
And those who keep
All in order.

A night for me
Of restless sleep,
Medical checks,
And waiting.

Normal life

For frontline staff,
An unusual night for
Me.

BIRDSONG II

The birds keep singing,
They always do,
Keep their songs close
A part of you.

Hold them tight,
Within your heart,
They'll get you through this
Right from the start.

ROBIN

A flash of red breast,
A flutter of wings,
From table to hedge
He gathers his things.
Hopping along
A mossy path,
He pecks at the ground
And gives me a laugh!

DUSK CHORUS

Unbidden, unseen,
The chirping begins
Chitter chatter
At close of day.
Polite homecomings,
They greet one another,
And prepare,
I presume,
For tomorrow.

PANDEMIC

Weary.
Depressed.
Stressed.
Tired.

Pandemic life:
Days
Good and bad.
Nights
Sketching nightmares.

Evening time wine:
Soothes.
Cools.
Relaxes.
Required.

Pandemic life:
Survived!

CHRISTMAS

Christmas cheer
This Covid year,
Is different for all
Far and near.

Time instead is
What we have,
As together we journey
Our unwelcome new path.

Time for reflection
On what has passed,
Anticipation and dread
For what lies ahead.

A glimpse of a future
We cannot see,
Together we hold tight
For whatever will be.

We will return
To this strange year,
In times ahead
That is clear.
Lessons learned now,

We'll bring as we travel
Into the future,
Which then we'll unravel.

Will we as a people
Have learned at all?
Or shall we become
Our own downfall...

THE HARDEST YEAR (2020)

The hardest year
Has come to pass,
2020 is over
At very long last.
What next year holds
We do not know,
But onwards we'll travel
Albeit slow.
Confined to the past
We'll one day leave masks,
Social distance and sanitizer
Thanks in no small part
To a vaccine from Pfizer.
It may take a while
To leave them behind,
But with our guiding light, Hope,
We'll bide our time.
2021 heralds a bright new future
A time to look forward,
To love
And to nurture.
It's been hard for us all
And will take time to recover,
But one day down the line
It'll all be over.

So look around:
Take in what you see,
And believe in your heart,
You'll soon be free.

THE HOUSE

It spoke to me,
Said love me,
Abandoned,
Needing human touch,
It found me.
Dirty floors,
Peeling walls,
A little love,
A little care,
Was all it called for.
In return,
It would reveal
All of its beauty,
Views in which
To roam free.
The house,
It called to me,
But Life,
Unfortunately,
Wouldn't allow me,
Couldn't indulge me,
Now it's just
Memory.
What might have been,
Had time been right for me!

But it was not to be,
I am sorry...

BALLYMACDERMOT

Those hills and skies,
And fields and lonesome roads,
That house and heather scented air.

Purple petals low reclined within
Mossy grass,
My roaming fingers lay bare.

The call of home,
It draws me near
The place I want to be.

My life
Tied to that family space,
Becomes my history.

FISH

(For Sarah)

What if
There's a fish
That has a higher
IQ than
Me?
Says my daughter.
What if there's a bird with
My personality?
I reply.
Who's to know
Or even care?
It matters not.
We are us;
We laugh,
We share
Thoughts of what may,
Or not,
Be there!

THE BIRD

A little bird
Watches me,
Perched on the edge
Of a windowsill.
In fading light
We both wait,
Watching the other,
Waiting to see
What?
My garden still
A velvet moth
Flutters past
Into the grass
As evening light dims.
The bird flits
To a fence,
Inching up on
Me,
But still I see
And silently watch
As he hops
Into my contorted hazel:
His tree.
No longer visible,
Almost imperceptible,

But the curled leaves rustle,
Betraying his place.
And maybe
He appraises me
As I turn quietly
Indoors
With but a slight glance
Behind me?
Nothing to see,
Save my reflection
In darkened glass.
Day turns to night,
As fast fades the light
Each getting on
With our own unique life...

I AM

I am me,
I live in here,
My self
Contained
Within
This frame.
Encased, embraced,
Alone I roam.
I am.

I am
Free,
At one with me,
Being
Who I need to be.

I am Life;
I live and breathe.
My soul alive.

I am.

RAIN

Standing at the window
In this strange new world,
Rain streams down.
Our day out,
Planned and perfected,
Dissolves.
Walking in rain soaked clothes
Used to be fun
When warming up, drying out
In a cosy cafe,
Supping hot tea,
Enjoying a scone
Or even breakfast,
Was promised.
But now,
Fear of the virus
Prevents all of us
Doing the things
That used to bring joy
To us.
How long this lasts
Cannot be foretold.
We wait,
We pray,
We hope for sun,

Anticipating fun,
But for now we keep safe
And dry, and warm,
By staying together
At home...

MUSE

I muse upon
My Muse.
Unseen, unknown.

At moments unplanned,
Thoughts and feelings
Crash forth
Tide like,
Flooding,
Compelling,
Requiring
Pen and page.
Creation cascades from
My stilled mind,
Whispered words softly fall
Into place.
I breathe them out
Gently.

Like old friends we unite,
Creating.
My Muse retreats,
The mist lifts,
And I am alone
Once more.

TIDES

Ripple sparkles
Reflect sunlight,
As rainbow bright
Pin people
Meander along
The receding shore.
Private thoughts
Stroll with them,
As salt air
Strokes fresh faces.
Tomorrow:
New people,
New thoughts,
Same tide
Repeats.

WATCHING

A perfect picnic
Takes place undisturbed
Distanced from all the others.
Soft breezes caress sun kissed
Cheeks
As castles of sand
Spring forth, unplanned.
Distant dogs delightedly
Chase far flung stones,
Sea water
Lapping at their paws.
Splats of red jellyfish flat
On warmed sand:
Like murder
Spread over the beach.
Buckets and spades,
Abandoned, forgotten
Delightful giggles
Dispersing worries and fears
Amidst sublime silent stillness.

A brightly coloured wind shield
Draws attention from
contented onlookers.
An unseen donkey brays

His foghorn warning
In the distance
Unnoticed.
Paddle boats
With children aboard
Bob gently,
Led by adults.
From a distance
The Lighthouse
Stands tall,
Sentry like,
Punctuating,
Guarding,
Observing:
Normal life unstoppable
Amidst it all.
A summer's day
In strange times.

22 JULY

(For Jack)
On this day
My midwife's voice
Moments after birth:
What have we here?
A little boy!
Too exhausted
To speak,
I smiled
My joy.
My little boy
Loved.
Dark hair,
Scrunched up face,
Velvet smooth skin,
I breathed you in.
Your eyes,
On mine.
Love
Innocent and true,
A promise
From me
To forever
Look after you...

WATERCOLOUR

Revealing itself
Before me,
A spectral watercolour
Splashes into life.
Coloured hills disappear
As sudden mist falls,
Then thickens,
Blotting the landscape.
Silhouetted trees meld into
Gentle hilltop spikes and curves,
Smoothed and soothed.

Illuminated by
Unseen sunshine,
The mist
Becomes rain,
Heavy splashes
Blurring my view
As a mountain
Disappears.
Amidst it all
Small boats
Sit still on the bay;
Silent witnesses
To Nature's artistry.

Off to my right
One boat floats,
Ghostlike,
An empty inflatable
Alongside it.
The painting complete,
The rain subsides,
The mist lightens, then lifts,
The colour returns
And my ghostly visage
Is gone.

APRIL 2021

(Day before my cancer diagnosis.)

it's clear
deep fear
takes hold
i grow old
my life
in your hands
i understand
my time here
hard to break
chains of tears
i am weary
life goes on all
around
i am bound
to keep walking
this life of mine
the chime of time
ignoring my
anxiety
set me free
let me be
i plea
darkness
falls

i grow cold
fear beats
in me
set me free...
i plea.

GOOD FRIDAY 2021

*(On being diagnosed with breast can
cer during the Covid 19 pandemic.)*

And they looked at me with
Compassion
And my chair shot across the room
Except it didn't
And I was lost in my own body
As they answered my question
Is it cancer?

THE FOREST

Forest bathing
In a sunlit wood,
An answered promise,
To lift the mood.

Rays of sun
Glint through tall trees,
A feast for the soul,
A gift for me.

SMALL STEPS

Walking.
One foot in front of another.
Breathing.
Again,
Again,
Again.
In and out,
In and out,
In and out.
Keep going.
Keep moving.
Keep watching.
Keep living.

GOD

I'm scared.

Don't be. I am with you.

Why me?

Why not.

I'm tired struggling.

Then stop. I will help you.

I need help.

Just ask me. I'm always here.

Everything has changed.

Everything does

Hold onto you and I'll hold you too.

S.E.C.T

Small. Early. Curable. Treatable:
4 positive words
To get me through
Weeks of worry
For me, for you.

Biopsies, surgery,
Therapies too?
I will do what
I have to do.

Life is more precious
Than ever before,
Each moment holds gifts
I now implore.

I sit still and breathe
And listen to sounds
Of people, of creatures,
Who pass by all around.

Precious moments come,
Unseen previously,
Bringing happy feelings,
Breathing fresh life into me.

ENEMY

Let me know my
Enemy,
So I can fight
Her off.

Let me know my
Enemy,
So I see her
Weaknesses and
Strengths.

Let me know my
Enemy,
So I prepare for the
Battle ahead.

Don't evade my questions,
Don't judge my ability to
Understand,
Let me have my
Answers.

For God's sake, please,
Let me know my
Enemy.

WALKING

Up the hill
And over the road,
Wearily carrying
My heaviest load.
The days stretch long
And far ahead,
Dark feelings trapped
Inside my head.
Chasing the sun
My future shines bright
I'll get through this time ,
And I'll be alright.

RAW WORDS

*One breast doesn't know the other has
cancer,*
*You must be a glass half empty type of
person,*
You don't have two tumours, only one,
*You can be a cancer survivor or a
cancer victim,*
*We all have cancer cells, you just
know where yours are!*

Aren't I lucky...
These are the words of 'support'
I received
From one who should have known better.

Call again anytime, she shrilled
Down the line
As I thanked her,
Hung up,
And said aloud to no one but myself,
'Not a chance...'

THE SURGEON

Momentarily,
The clock ticked
Louder,
Life got shorter,
Fear took over.
The surgeon spoke softly
A gentle caress,
Reassuring me
All would be fine,
And for me
No shortened timeline.
So now I breathe
Deeply,
Inhaling the air,
And rejoice in this life
That began afresh
With her.

AFTER

She slept
And she dreamt
That life was sweet
Again,
With red roses
And knee high
Grasses
And sunlit shadows
Days when life
Was fear free,
Just free…
And then
She turned,
Breathed deeply,
And time
Kept going
And she kept going
And she smiled
And she sighed
This is Life.

HEARTBEATS

My heart keeps beating,
And I keep breathing,
My life continues
And I am grateful
For the chance to travel
My journey.

LOSS

Losing a part of me
Hurt
Not just physically but
Deep to the core.
The loss
Forevermore.

EVERYTHING AND NOTHING

Everything I thought I knew,
I didn't.
Everything I thought I didn't,
I do.
Fear isn't what it was before:
It's raw, has teeth, and pounces
When least expected.
Love is deep and warm and soothes
With hugs and strokes in times of
need.
Despair empties you out
Right to the core;
It's tears and sobs and overwhelms.
But people all around, they care
More than I ever knew before,
With words that help and prayers that
heal...
These things I've learnt
And know and feel.

THE TREE

And so
The old tree
Sways over me
High up.

Blue
Peeps through
Fir fruitful branches
Whose arms
Lean down
To surround
My weary soul.

How many like me
Have been comforted
By this tree
Whose role today
Is just to mind me?
And remind me:
Just be.

CANCER TEARS

And when the
Tears fall
They don't stop
But trace a path:
Small streams,
Little rivers,
Racing
To pool
In a tissue
Scrumpled in my wet palm.
But after they've fallen
My light returns
And a tiny seed
Plants itself:
My future.
Small steps forward,
I embrace life,
Tears and all.

HOME TIME

Bags all packed
And ready to go,
Goodbye old tree
You watched over me so!

The sun is shining,
Puffed clouds glowing bright
Into this small room,
Reflecting sunlight.

Friendly faces
Waving me off,
Smiling faces
Bringing me home.

It's time to go,
To return to
My life,
And I'm ready for that...
Even the strife!

STEPPING FORWARD

A part of me is missing,
A part of me is sad,
For the life I never realised
That previously I had.

A part of me is happy,
A part of me relieved,
For the life that lies ahead now,
Knowing I am freed.

CANCER

And already I've met so many kind
people,
And my journey has just begun,
Fear meeting friendship,
Dulling the pain,
And unexpectedly,
Life looks good again.

TODAY

Today
Is the day
I celebrate life:
My life,
And your life.

Today,
I find peace
In the simple things,
Blessings before taken for granted:
A sunny seafront seat;
A sparkling drink in hand;
The people I love by my side;
Fresh air;
Clear skies.

Today,
I celebrate life.

LISTEN

Do you ever just sit
And listen
To birds chirping?
To the light summer
Breeze?
To cars humming by
On the road to somewhere?
To the bee in flight?
You should.

AFRESH

And tomorrow
I'll start afresh!
My cancer is
Gone,
Drug treatment
Begins,
And life starts over
Again.

DAY BY DAY

The fear still blinds
As I fall into sleep
And dreams so deep
I flail and wake
And cry and call
But time will heal
Or so I'm told.

I look in the mirror
And she looks back
At me
With tears in her eyes
The me I see.

I leave and smile
And chat and talk,
I hide behind
The confident walk.

Inside my head
I long to break free,
And travel back to
Embrace the old me.

Time has changed me,
My path took a turn,

But with it
I know
What I have learned
Life is precious
And sweet at times,
But it all can change
On the turn of a dime.

Grab it, enjoy it,
Make hay they say,
I'm learning to live now
Day by day.

ALL THE LOVE

You find out who cares
And who doesn't,
Just when you need them
The most.

The ones who spend time
Reaching out,
And then come the ones
Who don't
You may be surprised…
Or you won't.

Cancer has taught me some lessons,
My heart has been broken,
Then fixed,
My future is calling me forward,
The challenge is lifting
Those bricks.

The love that was shown
At my lowest,
Now rises within me
And leads,
As I look to the ones
Who helped me,

Right in my moments of need.

I'll carry my load
As intended,
I'll remember the love
That was shown,
This journey has been fraught
With fear,
But I haven't been travelling
Alone.

IT HURTS

Today,
It hurts
Not knowing
How long
I've got.

Hot tears
Fall free
None of us
Know
When our time
Is up,
But
It hurts,
A lot,
Today.

LIVING

Tears for the past
I have left behind,
Tears for the road
Ahead.

The moments come
As I sit alone,
And I live them,
And breathe them,
Then let them go.

FORMATION

Swooping and looping
A vanishing flock:
A fleeting glimpse
Of starlings in flight.

FRIENDS

Blackbird and sparrow,
Side by side,
Together they peck
At pickings dropped,
Circling each other,
Like two little friends.

DANDELIONS

Petals ablaze
In glorious gold
Like small suns.
Manes glowing
Across a universe
Of grass,
Daisies orbiting
Each and every one.

Garden time, alone.

LIFE

I write
And I sleep
And I dream
And I scream
And life comes
And it goes
And I'm scared
Then it passes
And I smile
And I chat
And I laugh
And I sing
And that's just
How life is
And that's just
What I love
And this life
Is mine
For whatever
Time.

CASTLEWELLAN

A cool wind
Drifts across
Choppy paddle boarded
Waters
As families picnic,
Dogs laze,
Strangers chat,
And children giggle
Welcome sounds
Following weeks of lockdown.

Energy bursts forth
As a lone child
Races herself
To the castle,
Then back,
Recording her delight
On a mobile.

Sun blistering heat
Breaks through
Dappled spaces
As we wander
A walled garden
And enjoy peaceful

Scenery
In abundance.

Ancient branches
Cast cooling shade,
Their long, smooth limbs
Reaching out,
Inviting climbing.

Too soon,
We return to the car;
Another day of
Memory making
Complete!

PIANO LESSONS

Muffled music escapes
From within
As a bee
Buzzes busily
By my open car window
On this warm summer's day.

Soothing sounds still me.

Happy birds
Chirp lazily
Hidden behind
Fruitful trees
Cloaked in shades of green.

An old stone wall
Has seen and heard it all
Many times
Before.

For me, it's the stuff
Of life
And I long for more.

CAR

Rain batters
Metal
As sitting in
Solitary
Silence
Creeping sadness
Threatens to
Overwhelm.
Tears pool in my eyes
As droplets follow unseen paths
Down the windscreen.
The beat of
The slow, steady, rain shower
Relaxes,
As breath slows and
My knot
Of melancholy
Unfurls.
Tomorrow the clouds
May clear,
The rain stop,
The mist lift,
The sun shine,
And life may sing
Once more.

MEMORIES

Memories of past
Happy times
Smiled at me from
My phone today.
Days of fun, laughing,
Eating out
Can we go back
To that easy freedom
Ever?
I hope,
I whisper,
I live.

TREE

Towering over me,
The old tree
Waves regally,
Biding her time,
As I pass mine.

Limbs stretched out
In lazy repose,
She watches and waits
As life comes and goes.

Who am I but
A momentary distraction?
Just one of many
Passing her by.

As each generation
Sees her grow tall,
From her height she
Looks down
Seeing it all.

We may think
We rule over our land,
But the earth is hers,

In the palm of her hand.

We, as a people,
Don't stay here long,
We walk, run, then tumble,
We are so small.

DEATH

(Words that came to me in a dream!)

    I wept for Irony the
    Night the Sun died,
    And now I feel
    Pain no more.

WAITING

A soft sun breeze sweeps my cheek
As chattering leaves shimmer
Beyond.

In a small border,
Tall flame flowers
Stand guard proudly
As a small patch of grass
Leans away from the light
Seeking refuge from the sweltering
heat.

Lazily, I observe,
And listen to my daughter
Singing through opened windows
On this hazy day.

A MORNING IN WARRENPOINT

The world is stilled
For a moment or more,
As Lough waves lap
Against the sea shore.

A small flock of birds
Low in flight,
Not quite skimming
Water
Oh what a sight!

A few hardy swimmers
Brave the fresh sea,
I watch and remark
That will never
Be me.

On a stone wall we sit
Entranced, hand in hand,
By soft misty mountains,
Lough water and land.

A few speeding cars
Disturb the peace,
Yet nothing can erase

Our love for this place.

RESULTS DAY

All masked up,
And lined up,
An envelope passed,
The contents of which
Reveal future paths.

Turn left or right,
A fork in the road!
Sciences, Arts,
Or perhaps a mixed load!

Whatever you choose,
Your future is beckoning,
The journey you embark on
Is of your own making.

Choose wisely,
Choose carefully,
This moment in Time
Is yours for the taking
All *will* work out fine...

A golden opportunity
Shines brightly today,
The choices you make,

Lead you on your way.

Stop for a moment,
Take a breath and recall,
Life stretches before you
Embrace it all...

PANDEMIC RESULTS

The results,
Long awaited,
Arrived
Revealing
Unexpected,
Upsetting grades,
Turning plans
Upside down,
Like life
In this time,
No reason or rhyme
Just comforting words,
Yet another
Side effect
Of the virus.

SATURDAY MORNING

On the pitch,
Hurls in hand,
Happy camogs,
On rain soaked land.

Giggles and smiles,
Aprons on,
Prepared for teamwork,
The sliotar is thrown.

The whack of wood,
The crack of the hurl,
The joy of play,
They're on their way!

Marking each other,
The race begins
To fight one another,
Be the team that wins!

The end of the challenge,
And victors rejoice:
Team mates forever,
They have one voice.
Leaving the pitch,

Game over, sticks in,
All huddled together
Small birds of a feather.

Off they wander,
Heading back home.
One battle lost,
Another won!

No matter the scor,
The fun remains,
Just a few days more
Until all starts again...

A MOMENT

A gentle breeze
Tickles skin
And flutters hair,
Ushering
Honeyed scent of wildflower
And warm tarmac.

Haloed clouds
Drift slowly,
Carefree,
Across pale blue sky
As sunlight
Shines bright through
Dark green leaves.

From below, I marvel at
Their soft luminescence.
A dove coos gently
Nearby, high, unseen.

In the cool shade
Of swaying poplars,
I sit and slowly breathe
Nature's calming touch
Punctuated only

By welcome birdsong.
This moment is mine.

AN EVENTFUL OCCASION

A Lockdown promise
Made to be kept,
A trip to McDonald's
Was due we all felt.

Masks on faces,
Hands sanitised,
Excitement gleaming
From bright young eyes.

In the queue we were asked
Take out or sit in?
Kids back to the car,
I ventured within.

Inside I struggled
Recalling each order,
The children's requests
Now but a blur.

Back in the car
In great expectations,
Empty tummies awaited
Their delectations.
All hell broke lose

And screaming ensued
Uninvited, a wasp joined us,
Tempted by our food!

Windows were opened,
Doors and boot too,
Bad news I'm afraid,
The wasp became two!

Coke spilt and profanities
Uttered aloud,
But at least we provided
Fun for the crowd!

I'll not hurry
To promise once more,
Next time it's delivery
To our own front door!

MORNING LIGHT

Where sea meets sky
And waves splash,
Sun lit water blinds
My eyes.
The fresh salty breeze
Sweeps the sea
Rushing to me
I breathe deeply.

This is Life.

HOME JOYS

Shower broken,
Sinks don't drain,
No phone signal
Feel my pain!
Taps turn on,
Then won't turn off,
I need a wash,
But can't have a bath.
How much more
Worse can it get?
Don't tempt fate,
It's not over yet.
The sooner, the better,
We get out of here
I scream aloud,
Please hear my prayer...

VIOLIN

Low September sun glows
Through my car window,
Tree shadows
Shape shift
Upon my skin.

Soft golden haze
Envelopes me,
A distant violin
Lullabies me.

Oh to sleep...

I close my eyes
Silence.

A JOURNEY

Words toss, turn,
Ripen and rush
To hungry page
And there they sit
As passengers
Awaiting full carriage.
The journey begins,
Pace quickens,
The story unfolds,
Is told,
By the end of the line.

AUTUMN

Twirling, drifting, floating,
Halting,
Swept
By an intermittent breeze,
In scattered circles,
Autumn leaves chase one another
Like children in a playground.
Yellows, reds and golden browns
Mingle,
Decaying matter,
Decaying together,
Their rich playful journey
Almost at an end,
Soon to feed the parent,
Anew, it starts again.

THE HUNNINGHAM OAK

Hunched,
Inside he weeps where
The ancient tree has been sliced.

Broken.

Life giving
Tree sap coats him.
The cost of progress,
The price of life.

WORDS WORDS WORDS

I've always loved
The journeys
My words have taken me on
Their many different meanings
From which creation spawns.
They fill me up with stories,
They flow from head to page,
They totter on the edge of life,
Their beauty ripe, uncaged.
I listen for the silence
Deep within my brain,
And wait for them to spill out,
For my journey to begin.
Words, words, words,
So many I've enjoyed,
A headful of forever friends,
Waiting to be deployed!

SCHOOL DAYS

I see myself in shadows,
Hear echoes of my laugh,
As passing through old corridors,
I mind how time has passed.

Those years went by so quickly,
Yet then they seemed so slow,
How fast it flies I wish I'd known,
Before, too soon, I was fully grown.

BATHTIME

Years of playtime,
In the bath,
Those well loved toys,
Their time now passed.
No longer needed,
It's time to let go,
But don't ever tell,
Or say I said so!
Another child will love and enjoy
Each very special little toy!
And so again they'll have their day,
In the bath for lots more play.

PANDEMIC

Strange times!
Strange times!
The words
Fall forth.

A common refrain,
Time and again,
As one and all,
We recall
Strange times indeed,
Paid with our greed,
For a life we did seed
And are used to.

Time for change,
The signs are clear,
But will we listen?
No, I fear...

CHILDREN

Smiles enshrined
In sunshine minds,
I glimpse within
And see their grins,
My little friends
Whom God did send!

HOME TIME

Waiting,
I watch
Children
Chatting and chasing
Through school gates
At the end of a long day.

My child races to me,
Smile wide on her face,
Today's news on her lips:
She won a prize
For best in class
At maths!

I look around
To check she's mine...
She didn't take after me
Numbers she got
From her daddy!

Together,
Homeward bound,
We chat
Amiably   that she got from me!

SCHOOL WALK

The walk to school,
Like so many others,
Is a chance to chat
And catch up.
Her small hand in mine,
Walking in time,
Breathing
The sweet morning air.
Traffic shoots past,
We cross roads fast,
And look at wildlife
On our way.
She stoops to save lives
Of snails on the path,
But slugs   no, they're too
Slimy and foul!
The early birds in the field,
She remarks,
Will catch worms,
And I know she has listened to me!
So much more fun
To walk there, then home,
Before each gets on
With our day.
Later we'll meet,

And the craic will be great,
And tomorrow will
Come round again.
These days I will miss
When they come to their end,
But I'll hold on for life
To the memories.
Someday we'll look back
On these school walks together,
And smile at the stories
We hold.
Those precious days
Will fill moments in time
The memories now
Are for then!

BIRD

A lone bird,
Atop a roof,
A dark silhouette
To my eye!
This shadow
Takes flight,
Disappears
Out of sight,
His purpose
Clear as the sky.

DEW

Dew tipped grass
Dagger like,
A world within
Balanced lightly
On the very edge of existence.
Soon sun burned off.
Tomorrow it begins again.

PARTY

Little tree, full of life
Year round
Invitations, white and gold
Sent out early Spring.
All partake,
The music starts
Buzzing and humming with life,
Your party,
A success for all,
Stretches into Summer!

Autumn,
Berry ripe,
A fat thrush sits regally
Upon his throne.
Sometimes, quietly,
A tiny bird disappears within,
The only clue
The slightest flicker
Of a branch.

Your Winter feast is legendary,
Your well earned rest is short,
Before again your invites
Scent the air.

MUFFIN

Fluffy,
Grey and white,
He sits
Under his favourite
Small tree
Like a rounded loaf of bread.

In *lump mode*,
My daughter's friend
Suggests,
He watches, waits,
Eyes darting,
Fur trembling,
Tail flicking,
With every movement.

At once,
Low and slow,
He stalks a prey
Unseen to me,
Hunting,
Chasing
Invisible air.

Once, he caught a bird,

Sat on it,
Unsure what to do.
The bird escaped
A most unsuccessful hunter!

So he sits,
Still, silent,
Awaiting another fruitless encounter.

That's our cat!

SHOPPING

Empty shopping malls,
These are our times...
Silence stretched
Across newly marked lines.
Stay left,
We are ordered,
With a mask on your face,
Keep hands sterile
In each new space.
This is life now,
Our new wondrous land,
So we each try
To do what we can
To keep ourselves safe
In this bewildering place.

FIRST HOLY COMMUNION

Excitement before the
Big Day ahead,
A little girl tucked up
In her cosy bed.

In the morning,
Before the event,
To the hairdresser,
With mummy she went.

Prettied and preened,
Stepping into white dress,
She smiles in the mirror,
Admiring herself.

Soon off to the church
With her family
She goes,
And on the seat places
White bag and white gloves.

Photos and smiles,
Then seated she waits,
Soon she'll receive
The Sacrament.
Filled with love from Jesus,

She leaves,
Life starting over again,
She breathes.

BEAUTY

I see beauty
In the upturned, dew filled rose petal
Littering my lawn.

I see beauty in soaked grass reaching
for the sky.

I see beauty in the red breasted robin
Hopping from branch to branch.

Do they see beauty in me?

EVER AFTER

We live,
We die.
In between
To us belongs.
Beyond,
Not so.

Here and Now
Is all we have,
The ever after
In hope,
We go.

SURVIVING

There's a tightness
In my chest
I find difficult
To express
Fear running free,
Racing through me.
Better days will come,
Bright will shine the sun,
And life will go on...

BREATHLESS

On Winter hardened soil,
Delicate bell like petals
On Long stalks bearing
Snowdrops appear
Heralding brighter days ahead
As now
We wait,
Watch,
Want,
Crave,
The long gone freedom light
Of yesteryears.
We hold tight
As they.
This discontent will pass
And our Spring
Return
And how we'll rejoice
In togetherness.

LOSING THE SKY

From my favourite seat,
The sky disappears
Day by day,
Brick by brick,
No longer a view
Of wide open fields
A far off tree waves
Farewell to me,
As my world closes in,
Becomes life in a box.

FRICTION

A car pulls up
And from
Outside,
I hear the fight
Within:

A teenage girl
And her mum
At war,
What is all the
Arguing for?

I cannot help
But quietly smile,
As head bowed low
I reconcile:
So it's not just me!

And I feel for her
As the car revs up
And pulls away.
Another fight,
Another day!

SKY

There's a hole in the
Sky
Where the blue
Peeps through
And below it
I sit
And I wonder why
The clouds interfere
And get in the way
Of what could be
A beautiful day.

A WINDY DAY

Like waves,
Hushed wind howls
Through creaks and cracks.
Trees,
As boats,
Sway side to side
Riding oceans unseen;
Wooden flags steering
A stationary course.

Raindrops
Pool,
Stream,
Soak
Through
Fields and rivers
Making haste to sea;
Where dead wood
Floats
Alive with living.

WAITING II

Softly swishing distant trees,
Dancing together,
To an unheard lovesong,
Effortlessly blending
With the soothing hum
Of far off traffic and
The whirl of helicopter blades.

Low swooping birds,
Dipping, diving,
Flitting fleetingly,
Joyfully,
Dancing across
Fresh cut, dew soft grass.

Ahead,
Bubbles of fertile trees fence off
Tranquil rolling
Patchwork hills.
My watching eyes see
As warm air breathes
Welcome life into me.

All around,
Living free,

These things happen,
And please me.

AFTER HALLOWE'EN

Silent and still,
In evening light,
I deeply inhale
Chill
Autumn air:
One slow, deep, breath
To lull, cleanse, refresh,
And my words flow forth
Once more.

TIME

i find a quiet spot
in my mind
tune out
and unwind
this time is mine
here I feel fine
relaxed and
at peace
and free
to be me

TALKING

(For Julie)

She sits
And she waits
For me to talk,
And words that were hidden
Spill fast,
Releasing fears through tears
That have held on tight,
That have pulled me back,
Stopped my journey
Mid track.

She smiles
And she tells me
It's normal and fine,
And her warmth
Wraps around me tight,
As from her small room
She offers a gift:
Permission to scream, laugh,
Cry and shout,
Permission to feel what
Life's all about.

Her calm, quiet air

Encapsulates me,
And now I feel light,
Released and free
From the internal cage
That imprisoned me.

FAITH

I will shine my brightest
Rays of light,
And you will feel me there.
Always I am with you,
Feel me in your prayer.

SMALL THINGS

Welcome them in,
The small things:
Revel in the blackbird's song,
The business of the bee,
The twitter of the sparrow,
The heat of the sun
On bare skin,
And live this life
It might be
Your only one.

JUST BE

Drink the sunshine,
Inhale the breeze,
Sit still for a moment
And let it all be.

ABOUT THE AUTHOR

Sinéad Hoben

 Sinéad Hoben lives in Northern Ireland with her husband and 4 children. She attended the University of Ulster, graduating with BA(Hons)English followed by PGCE English and Drama with Media. Having worked as an English teacher for several years, she became a stay at home mum following the birth of her second child. Writing has always been important to Sinéad and she has written and published several books for children. She has also written short articles for a number of online publications.